I0504077

THIS JOURNAL BELONGS TO

www.ingramcontent.com/pod-product-compliance
Lightning Source LLC
Chambersburg PA
CBHW030720220526
45463CB00005B/2121
* 9 7 8 1 6 9 0 1 3 1 0 7 6 *